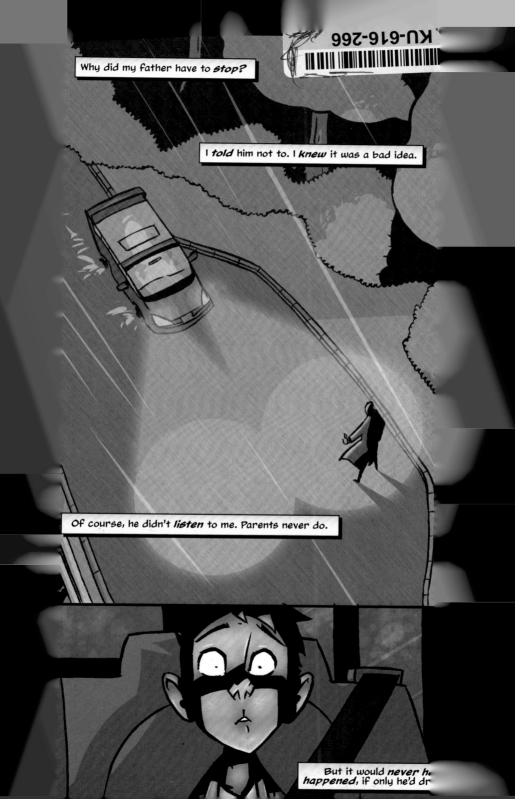

THE
HITCHHIKER

ANTHONY HOROWITZ

ADAPTED BY TONY LEE • ILLUSTRATED BY DAN BOULTWOOD

First published in 2010
by Franklin Watts

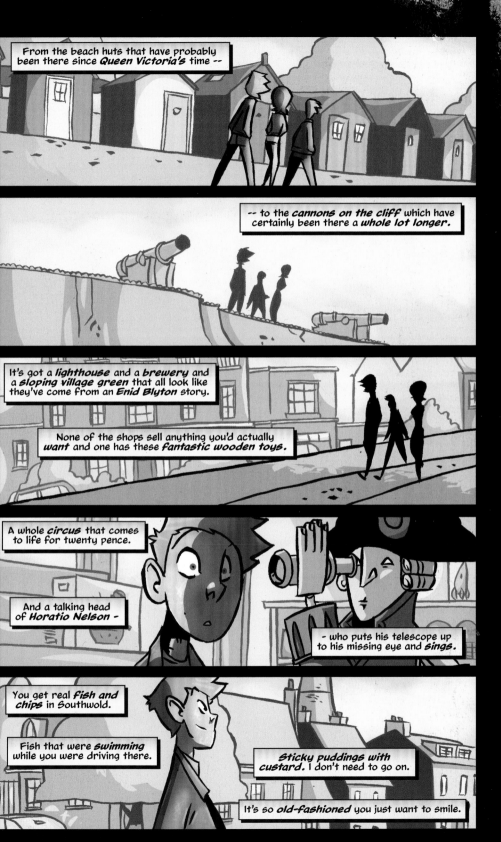

From the beach huts that have probably been there since *Queen Victoria's* time --

-- to the *cannons on the cliff* which have certainly been there a *whole lot longer.*

It's got a *lighthouse* and a *brewery* and a *sloping village green* that all look like they've come from an *Enid Blyton* story.

None of the shops sell anything you'd actually *want* and one has these *fantastic wooden toys.*

A whole *circus* that comes to life for twenty pence.

And a talking head of *Horatio Nelson* -

- who puts his telescope up to his missing eye and *sings.*

You get real *fish and chips* in Southwold.

Fish that were *swimming* while you were driving there.

Sticky puddings with custard. I don't need to go on.

It's so *old-fashioned* you just want to smile.

And then it was time to leave.

Come on Jacob! *Five pm!* Time to go before we hit the *traffic!*

Look at that, John - now *that's* a real Suffolk sunset.

The sky was pink and grey and dark blue -

- and there was almost *too much* of it.

You know that strange, *heavy* feeling you get at the end of a really good day?

I'm sad it's all over. But glad too, you know?

Looks like we timed it right -

- it's starting to *rain.*

6

It was an hour's drive, and by the time we reached the **A12** it was raining heavily.

Look at the *rain come down!*

I'd hate to be walking in it like *that* poor fellow!

I wonder where he's going?

My older brother, *Eddy*. He *died* suddenly when he was twelve years old.

An *accident* --

-- he fell underneath a *speeding train.*

That was *nine years ago* - and my parents have *never* really recovered.

I miss him too.

Of course, he bullied me now and then - like *all* big brothers do --

-- but his death was a *terrible* thing.

It hurt us all - and we knew that the pain would *never* go away.

Where are you going?

Ipswich.

That's *twenty miles* away!

But in *this weather* that'll take *hours.*

My car's *broken down* - I'm heading there on foot.

Well - we're heading that way. We can give you a lift!

John --

There was a *reason* for Mum's concern.

The A12 is a **long, dark road** often with no buildings in sight. There weren't even any **street lights.**

It's the one place in the world where you'd have to be **crazy** to pick up a stranger --

Thanks.

-- because it's only **ten miles** from **Fairfields.**

Because, you see, **everyone** knows about **Fairfields.**

It's a big, ugly building not far from Woodbridge, surrounded by a wall that's **fifteen metres high** with spikes along the top -

- and **metal gates** that open electronically.

The **name** is quite new.

It used to be called the **East Suffolk Maximum Security Prison for the Criminally Insane.**

So, what's your name?

Rellik. Ian Rellik. Is this your son here in the back?

Yes! That's our Jacob! He's fifteen years old today! Can you *believe* it!

It's his birthday?

Happy *birthday*, Jacob.

I took the hand. It was like holding a *dead fish.*

Thank you.

I glanced down and saw that his *sleeve* had pulled back - exposing his *wrist.*

What do you do?

Me? I'm a **dentist.**

Really? I haven't seen a dentist...

...not for a **very long** time.

You should go **twice a year!**

You're right. I should.

John! Pay attention to the road! Please!

Dental hygiene isn't something to be **ignored,** dear!

21

HAHAHAHAHAHA!!

Are you a *vampire*, Mister Rellik?

Where do you want us to drop you?

Anywhere.

Well - where do you *live* in Ipswich?

There was a *pause.*

Blade Street.

...

He *paused* before answering her question.

He said it so quietly that only I had heard, and this time I *knew* for certain.

He was *mad*.

I'm going to *kill* you.

He'd escaped from *Fairfields*.

We had picked him up in the middle of *nowhere* and he was going to *kill us all*.

And that was when I happened to look into the *driver's mirror*.

I'd written *Rellik* on the window moments before –

– but reflected in the *mirror*, it said something else.

HAHAHAHAHA!!!!

-- or *worse.*

My parents didn't know *anything* -

- but for some reason the man had made himself *known* to me.

You're going to *die.*

You're going to join your *brother.* In *Hell.*

So what *were* my choices?

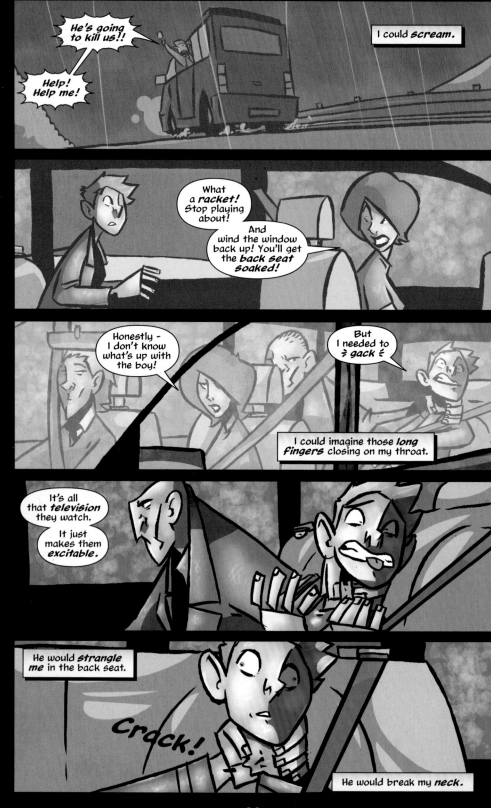

30

And my parents would drive on without even knowing what had *happened* to me --

-- until it was *their* turn.

DIIIIEEEEE!!!!

No. *That* wouldn't work.

I could *trick* him.

Wurgh - I don't feel well!

What's the matter?

I - I feel *car sick!*

I think I'm gonna *throw up!* Like *right now!*

33

The car would go out of *control.*

CRASH!

AAARRGHHHH!!!!

SPLOOOOSHH.!!

I knew *exactly* what was going to happen.

DIIIIEEEEE!!!!

He would *attack* me. My father would stop the car.

Then it would be *his* turn. And then my *mother's*.

I got myself into position - my shoulders pressed into the side of the car to give me *leverage*.

Mister Rellik had made a *bad mistake*.

With his hand under his jacket, he couldn't *defend himself*.

What --

YEEAAAAHHH!!!!

Both my feet *slammed* into him --

Nooo --

SCREEEEEECH!!!

What --

He was gonna *kill* us, Dad!

He had a *knife* and he came from *Fairfield* and his name was *Rellik* which is *killer* backwards --

-- and there was *blood* on his hands -

- and he didn't live here and Blade Street doesn't *exist* and I *had* to save us!

Oh God - *Oh God* --

Wait here.

It's *all right,* Jacob.

I could see out of the back window.

My father spoke to the lorry driver. There wasn't any sign of *Mister Rellik*.

He must have been spread out over a *fair bit* of the A12.

It had been *horrible*, what had happened –

– but I wasn't *afraid* anymore. I had done what I *had* to do.

I had *saved* both my parents and myself.

We should never have stopped. *Never*.

He's going to call the *police*. We're nearly there, so I said we'd go on.

I've given him our details.

Did you tell him what happened?

Yes. He knows you did the *right thing*, Jacob.

Don't worry. We're going to leave now.

We drove for another ten minutes and then, just past the first sign to Woodbridge –

– we turned down a narrow lane.

After a mile, we came to a high brick wall with spikes. I *knew* where we were.

We had come to *Fairfields*.

The *East Suffolk Maximum Security Hospital for the Criminally Insane.*

My father had to tell them what *happened*, of course.

He'd agreed that with the lorry driver.

Why are we *here*, Dad? Is it because Rellik came from Fairfields?

Is it to tell them what happened? How he tried to *kill us* and we had to act in *self-defence?*

Yes, Jacob. That's why we're here.

Wait here with your mother.

Later, they told me that the hitchhiker's name was Mister *Renwick* -

- and that I'd *misheard* him.

Apparently he was a *gardener* who had been working outside Lowestoft.

His car had broken down and he'd *hitchhiked* as far as Southwold --

-- where *we* picked him up.

They told me that it was *mud* I had seen on his wrist -

- not *blood*.

And that when they had scraped him off the *tarmac*, he had been holding not a *knife* -

- but a *cigarette case*.

44

That was what they *told* me - but I didn't believe *any* of it.

After all - they *also* told me a lot of lies after my *brother Eddy* fell under that train.

You'll never bully me again, Eddy!

They even wanted me to believe that *I'd* pushed him!

So here I am, back in my *room*. Looking out of the window at the *same old view.*

I had such a *nice day* in Southwold.

I just hope I won't have to wait *another nine years* before they take me out again.

End.

ANTHONY HOROWITZ

Anthony's mum used to read him horror stories when he was eight years old, and this is the inevitable result. He has been called the busiest writer in England and is best known for his ALEX RIDER novels which have sold over twelve million copies worldwide. He used to write in a garden shed until his wife sold the garden. Now he lives and works in London.

TONY LEE

Tony has been writing for over twenty years, and has worked on X-MEN, SPIDER MAN and recently DOCTOR WHO for IDW. His graphic novel OUTLAW: THE LEGEND OF ROBIN HOOD for Walker Books was on the ALA 'Best of 2010' list. Tony is also adapting Anthony Horowitz's POWER OF FIVE series for Walker Books.

DAN BOULTWOOD

Dan has illustrated several critically acclaimed graphic novels, including THE GLOOM and HOPE FALLS for Markosia, THE PRINCE OF BAGHDAD for Random House and G.P. Taylor's THE DOPPLEGANGER CHRONICLES for Tyndale Press.

THE HITCHHIKER by Anthony Horowitz was originally published in a short story collection by Orchard Books. Check out all the frightfully good HOROWITZ HORROR titles at: www.orchardbooks.co.uk

Abandon hope...

ANTHONY
HOROWITZ
HORROR
2

WHATEVER YOU DO, DON'T TURN OFF THE LIGHT...

Other HOROWITZ GRAPHIC HORROR titles:

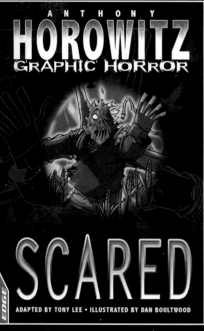

978 0 7496 9511 8

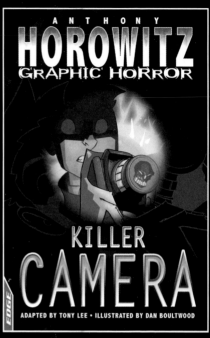

978 0 7496 9510 1

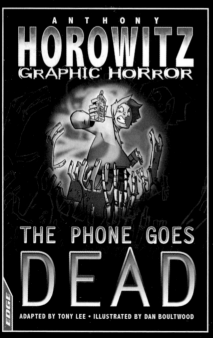

978 0 7496 9509 5

For more information
about the latest hot
releases from EDGE
log on to:
www.franklinwatts.co.uk
and click on our link.

LONDON·SYDNEY